n Forest Libraries

‖‖‖ ‖‖ ‖‖‖‖ ‖‖‖‖‖ ‖‖‖‖‖‖‖‖‖ ‖‖‖‖

stamped. The l
her customer

✔ KT-381-700

WALTHAM FOREST LIBRARIES

904 000 00406751

Fiction
at this level

FISHING FOR **TROUBLE**
DAVID and HELEN ORME
978 1 4451 1812 3 pb

FOOTBALL **LEGEND**
DAVID and HELEN ORME
978 1 4451 1813 6 pb

VAMPIRES ARE **SO BORING**
DAVID and HELEN ORME
978 1 4451 1813 0 pb

MY NAME IS **COLEN**
STEVE BARLOW and STEVE SKIDMORE
978 1 4451 3070 5 pb

DEVIL'S **TEETH**
STEVE BARLOW and STEVE SKIDMORE
978 1 4451 3054 5 pb

SPACE STATION ALERT
DAVID and HELEN ORME
978 1 4451 3068 2 pb

Graphic fiction
at this level

DEMON **STREAK**
JONNY ZUCKER with STEVE SAMPSON
978 1 4451 1799 7 pb

FULL METAL **HERO**
JONNY ZUCKER with DAN BOULTWOOD
978 1 4451 1801 7 pb

TERROR **BEAST**
JONNY ZUCKER with MACK CHATER
978 1 4451 1800 0 pb

ALIEN **ACADEMY**
JONNY ZUCKER with IVAN PENTNEY
978 1 4451 3088 0 pb

DOWNHILL **RACERS**
JONNY ZUCKER with IAIN BUCHANAN
978 1 4451 3089 7 pb

BEYOND THE **WALL**
JONNY ZUCKER with TOMAS ARANDA
978 1 4451 3090 3 pb

Non-fiction
at this level

BUILDINGS
ANNE ROONEY
978 1 4451 1952 6 hb
978 1 4451 3229 7 pb

CRAZY **FOOD**
ANNE ROONEY
978 1 4451 1954 0 hb
978 1 4451 3228 0 pb

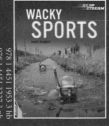

WACKY **SPORTS**
ANNE ROONEY
978 1 4451 1953 3 hb
978 1 4451 3227 3 pb

AMAZING **PETS**
ANNE ROONEY
978 1 4451 3050 7 hb

DANGEROUS **EARTH**
ANNE ROONEY
978 1 4451 3052 1 hb

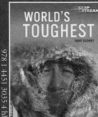

WORLD'S **TOUGHEST**
ANNE ROONEY
978 1 4451 3035 4 hb

SLIP STREAM

WORLD'S TOUGHEST

ANNE ROONEY

EDGE
FRANKLIN WATTS

LONDON · SYDNEY

Waltham Forest Libraries

S

904 000 00406751	
Askews & Holts	25-Jul-2014
C620.112 ROO	£8.99
4368784	

First published in 2014 by
Franklin Watts
338 Euston Road
London NW1 3BH

Franklin Watts Australia
Level 17/207 Kent Street
Sydney NSW 2000

© Franklin Watts 2014

(hb) ISBN: 978 1 4451 3035 4
(Library ebook) ISBN: 978 1 4451 3036 1

Dewey classification number: 620.1'12

All rights reserved

The right of Anne Rooney to be
identified as the author of this Work
has been asserted in accordance
with the Copyright, Designs and
Patents Act, 1988.

A CIP catalogue record for this book
is available from the British Library.

Series Editors: Adrian Cole and Jackie Hamley
Series Advisors: Diana Bentley and Dee Reid
Series Designer: Peter Scoulding
Designer: Cathryn Gilbert
Picture Researcher: Diana Morris

Printed in China

Franklin Watts is a division of
Hachette Children's Books,
an Hachette UK company.
www.hachette.co.uk

Acknowledgements:
C Barnes Photography/Getty Images: 9.
Sepp Friedhaler/istockphoto: 11.
Gefobob/Dreamstime: 19.
Gentoomultimedia/Dreamstime: 4b, 10.
Julien Gronden/Dreamstime: 14.
Gulustan/Wikipedia: 20.
JPL/NASA: 22.
Steve Kazlowski/Getty Images: front cover, 5.
Ladiras81/Dreamstime: 4t, 16.
Larentin Lordache/Dreamstime: 18.
Dimitri Lovetsky/AP/PAI: 7.
Evgeny Moglinikov/Shutterstock: 6.
NASA/Carnegie Mellon University/SPL: 15.
Paramount Group www.paramountgroup.biz:
1, 21.
Science Picture Co/Superstock: 12.
Sovfoto/Getty Images: 23.
Sinclair Stammers/SPL: 8.
Travelling Light/Dreamstime: 17.
Stefanie Winkler/Dreamstime: 13.

Kevlar® is a registered trademark of
E. I. du Pont de Nemours and Company
or its affiliates.

Every attempt has been made to
clear copyright. Should there be any
inadvertent omission, please apply
to the publisher for rectification.

CONTENTS

TOUGH STUFF

Tough trucks pull heavy loads.
Tough ships smash through ice.

Tough people like the Inuit live where the ground is frozen and nothing grows.

TOUGH HELICOPTER

This is the toughest helicopter in the world.
It is called the Mi—26.

It can lift heavy
loads like this jet.

TOUGH MATERIAL

Kevlar® is the toughest man-made material in the world. It is stronger than steel.

It is used to make body
armour, tyres and the
cables that hold up bridges.

TOUGH SHIP

This ship breaks through ice. It smashes a path for other ships. It has a very powerful engine and a strong hull.

TOUGH LIFE

A water bear is just 1 mm long. It can live without food or water for months.

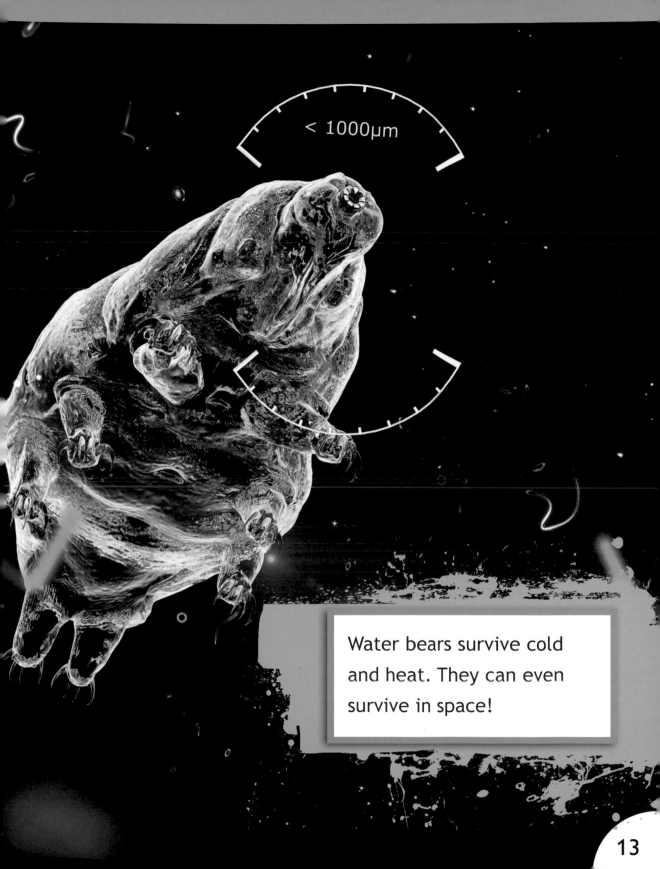

< 1000μm

Water bears survive cold
and heat. They can even
survive in space!

TOUGH ROBOT

A tough robot called Dante explores volcanoes.
It even crawled inside a volcano.

TOUGH ENGINE

This tough engine pulls trailers and is called a 'road train'. The trailers are loaded with heavy goods.

Road trains can weigh more than 100 tonnes. That is very heavy!

TOUGH SPIDERS

The toughest natural fibre is made by spiders.
Spiders make silk for webs and nests.

36 ►

NEGATIVE 35 mm

35

For its size, spider silk is as strong as high-grade steel.

TOUGH TRUCK

This truck is so tough it can drive through a wall. The truck helps to keep people inside it safe from bombs.

TOUGH JOURNEY

The Venera 7 probe landed on the planet
Venus. It travelled over 38 million kilometres.
The temperature on Venus is over 460 °C.

INDEX

FOR TEACHERS

About

Slipstream is a series of expertly levelled books designed for pupils who are struggling with reading. Its unique three-strand approach through fiction, graphic fiction and non-fiction gives pupils a rich reading experience that will accelerate their progress and close the reading gap.

At the heart of every Slipstream non-fiction book is exciting information. Easily accessible words and phrases ensure that pupils both decode and comprehend, and the topics really engage older struggling readers.

Whether you're using Slipstream Level 2 for Guided Reading or as an independent read, here are some suggestions:

1. Make each reading session successful. Talk about the text before the pupil starts reading. Introduce any unfamiliar vocabulary.

2. Encourage the pupil to talk about the book using a range of open questions. For example, what tough stuff do they think is most useful? Why?

3. Discuss the differences between reading non-fiction, fiction and graphic fiction. Which do they prefer?

For guidance, SLIPSTREAM Level 2 – World's Toughest has been approximately measured to:

National Curriculum Level: 2b
Reading Age: 7.6–8.0
Book Band: Purple

ATOS: 2.5*
Guided Reading Level: I
Lexile® Measure (confirmed): 570L

*Please check actual Accelerated Reader™ book level and quiz availability at www.arbookfind.co.uk